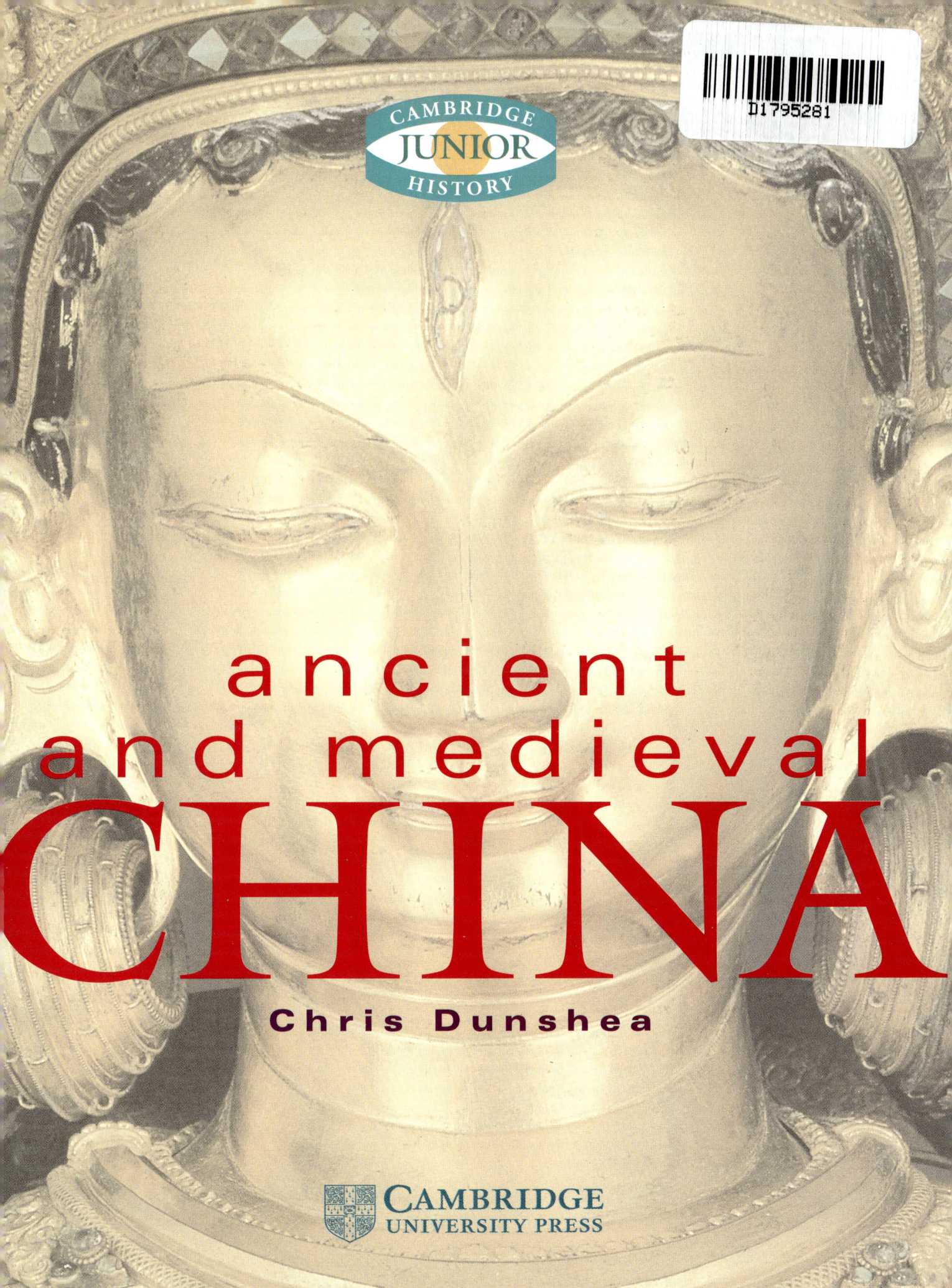

CAMBRIDGE
JUNIOR
HISTORY

ancient
and medieval
CHINA

Chris Dunshea

CAMBRIDGE
UNIVERSITY PRESS

PUBLISHED BY THE PRESS SYNDICATE OF THE UNIVERSITY OF CAMBRIDGE
The Pitt Building, Trumpington Street, Cambridge, United Kingdom

CAMBRIDGE UNIVERSITY PRESS
The Edinburgh Building, Cambridge CB2 2RU, UK
40 West 20th Street, New York, NY 10011–4211, USA
10 Stamford Road, Oakleigh, VIC 3166, Australia
Ruiz de Alarcón 13, 28014 Madrid, Spain
Dock House, The Waterfront, Cape Town 8001, South Africa

http://www.cambridge.org

First published 2001

Printed in Singapore by Green Giant Press

Typeface Berkeley 11.5/14 pt
System QuarkXPress 4.04®

National Library of Australia
Cataloguing in Publication data
    Dunshea, Christopher
    Ancient & medieval China

    Includes index
    ISBN 0 521 77650 3 paperback

1. China — Civilization — Juvenile literature.
I. Title. (Series : Cambridge junior history).

952

ISBN 0 521 77650 3

Contents

Introduction and outcomes

In this book, you will be learning about the civilisations of ancient and medieval China. You will be using a variety of sources to achieve the following outcomes.

Knowledge and understandings

By the end of this book, you should be able to:

- Identify the chronology of events in Chinese history.
- Describe some of the main features of Chinese society.
- Describe the major issues, personalities, events and cultural groups of Chinese history.
- Describe the way that different cultures have developed independently and in communication with each other.
- Describe the different experiences of citizenship of Chinese people throughout their history.

Skills

By the end of this book, you should be able to:

- Use historical terms relating to ancient and medieval China in appropriate contexts.
- Identify the meaning, context and purpose of historical sources in order to draw basic conclusions about how we can use them to answer specific questions about ancient and medieval China.
- Recognise different perspectives and sometimes bias — about individuals, groups, events and issues, with some help from your teacher.

- Locate, evaluate, select and organise historical information from a variety of sources to address historical problems and issues.
- Express your ideas orally.
- Present material to an audience graphically and in written form.

Inquiry questions

In achieving these outcomes, you will be exploring the following inquiry questions:

- What were the origins of ancient and medieval Chinese society?
- How do we know about ancient and medieval China?
- What were some of the major features of ancient and medieval Chinese society?
- How were the ancient and medieval Chinese governed?
- What were the beliefs and values of the ancient and medieval Chinese?
- What contact did the ancient and medieval Chinese have with other peoples?
- What has ancient and medieval China contributed to the modern world?

Text types

You will also be exploring the following text types within this book:

- Retelling history
- Describing history
- Explaining history
- Arguing history.

RUSSIAN FEDERATION

KAZAKHSTAN

KYRGYZSTAN

TAJIKISTAN

PAKISTAN

INDIA

NEPAL

BHUTAN

MYNAMAR

THAILAND

LAOS

VIETNAM

MONGOLIA

Lake Baikal

Lake Balkhash

Urumqi

XINJIANG

TIBET

QINGHAI

GANSU

NINGXIA

Lanzhou

Baotou

Huang He (Yellow)

Huang He

INNER MONGOLIA

HEILUNGKIANG

Qiqihar

Harbin

Changchun

Jilin

JILIN

LIAONING

Shenyang

Fushun

Anshan

Dalian

Tangshan

NORTH KOREA

SOUTH KOREA

JAPAN

Sea of Japan

Yellow Sea

Qingdao

Jinan

SHANDONG

Huang He

Beijing

Tianjin

HEBEI

Shijiazhuang

Handan

Taiyuan

SHANXI

Zhengzhou

Luoyang

HENAN

Suzhou

Kuzhou

ANHUI

Nanjing

JIANGSU

Shanghai

Hangzhou

Wenzhou

ZHEJIANG

Chang Jiang

Nanchang

JIANGXI

FUJIAN

Fuzhou

East China Sea

TAIWAN

Pacific Ocean

PHILIPPINES

South China Sea

Kowloon
HONG KONG

Guangzhou

GUANGDONG

HAINAN

Xi Jiang

Nanning

GUANGXI

YUNNAN

Kunming

GUIZHOU

Guiyang

Neijiang

Chongqing

SICHUAN

Chengde

Changde

Yueyang

Changsha

HUNAN

HUBEI

Wuhan

SHAANXI

Xi'an

Chang Jiang

Chiang Jiang (Yangtze)

Mekong

Nu Jiang (Salween)

Yarlung Zangbo Jiang

Brahamaputra

Chindwin

Bay of Bengal

500 km

0

1-1

China today

City and country life

1

In this chapter, you will be investigating the following issues:
- What were the geographical features of China?
- How did ancient and medieval Chinese city and country people live?
- What were the principal industries of ancient and medieval China?

Geography

In ancient times, the Earth's climate was warmer than it is today, and the wide river valleys of China were covered with forests and marshes. Boar, deer, panthers, wolves, leopards, elephants, tigers and rhinoceros roamed the countryside.

China's landscape consists mainly of mountains and plateaus with rivers that run from west to east. The physical barrier of the mountains meant that many small regional populations developed and that each had their own customs.

The most important river in China is the Huanghe River, which is also known as the Yellow River. 'Huang tu' means 'the yellow earth'. The soil that gives the river its yellow colour is called 'loess'. Loess is fine, stone-free, yellow soil that can be up to 75 metres in depth. The earliest field agriculture was in this 'loess' soil of the Yellow River valley.

The Yellow River was also known as 'China's sorrow' because of the frequency with which it flooded and devastated the surrounding areas.

Eventually a Grand Canal was built to join the Yellow River and the Chang Jiang (once known as the 'Great River' or the 'Long River'). The local people in the province of Jiangsu called the river the Yangtze.

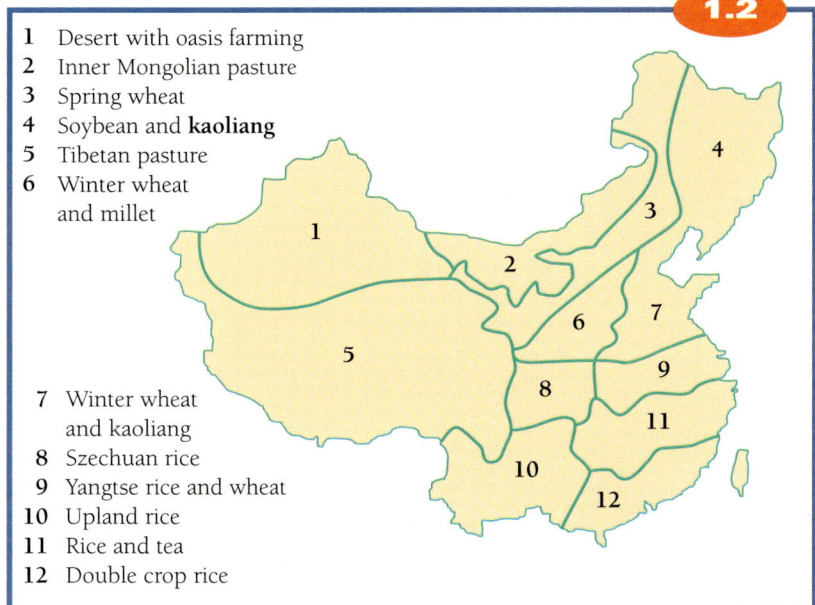

1.2

1 Desert with oasis farming
2 Inner Mongolian pasture
3 Spring wheat
4 Soybean and **kaoliang**
5 Tibetan pasture
6 Winter wheat and millet
7 Winter wheat and kaoliang
8 Szechuan rice
9 Yangtse rice and wheat
10 Upland rice
11 Rice and tea
12 Double crop rice

Agricultural districts

Using the information

Look carefully at the map of China (source 1.1 on page iv) and find the following places on the map. Find information in your library on three of these, and write short notes on each:
1 Xian
2 The Chang Jiang
3 Tibet
4 Beijing
5 Huang He
6 Mongolia
7 Huangzhou
8 Louyang.

kaoliang   a variety of grain

Daily life

Towns were built to a pattern. Each town had a granary and walls were made of earth that was packed solid and supported with wood or bamboo.

The palace of a prince was built in the centre of the town near the market and the houses of officials and workshops for craftspeople were to the south.

Han cities were built on a north-south axis and planned on a grid system. A system of **corvee** meant that, between the ages of 23 and 56, men could be required to work on the construction of buildings or serve in the army.

Housing

Models of houses in tombs from Han times show that houses included:
*   multi-level houses for the rich
*   houses on stilts in swamps.

The houses of the rich were rectangular in shape and supported by wooden pillars. The outside roof timbers were colourfully painted and windowpanes were oiled paper not glass. 'Gate Gods' protected the gates of the house. Much of the furniture in the house, including the beds, was painted with black **lacquer**.

Feng shui (wind and water) was a method of positioning a building so that it did not offend the spirit of the site and so promoted **harmony** and **prosperity** for those living in it.

In poor districts, many families lived in one house. Houses were sometimes just one room with a stable or shed attached. In medieval China, some housing was government owned and the rent was fixed according to how many people lived there.

1.3

Farmhouse

corvee	working for the government or an overlord	**harmony**	being in agreement
lacquer	tree sap used as a varnish	**prosperity**	wealth, success, good fortune

Researching the past

Using the Internet and your library, research more information on the styles of housing throughout Chinese history. Try these web sites:
http://www.hcc.hawaii.edu/hcconline/draft26/general/fengshui.htm
http://www.astro-fengshui.com/FengShui/wuxing.htm

Food

Chinese people ate vegetables and rice, rice wine and cakes. In the north they also ate millet and wheat products. Chopsticks and porcelain bowls were the main eating utensils.

In the thirteenth century (AD 1200s) people began to use tea leaves in hot water. There were six kinds of Chinese tea: red, black, green, Wuloong, flower and brick.

Other foods included soya beans and bean curd or *doufu* (tofu). Beans were a source of protein. There were many Chinese spices including ginger. Food was preserved by drying it in the sun.

Money

In Han times, a rectangular copper five-shu piece was used as money. The five-shu piece had a hole in the middle so that a number of coins could be tied together.

Copper coins were made in bronze moulds. In the Han Dynasty, copper coins were easily forged at first. So, to overcome this, the coin was made worth the value of the metal. In the Tang Dynasty, paper certificates were issued for government purchases.

Paper money was printed and widely used after AD 1024 and the idea of using paper money spread to Mongolia, Persia, Korea and Japan.

Clothing

Clothing was a mark of class in China. **Hemp**, not wool, was used to make clothes and silk was also used. A hat always showed the wearer's occupation and status, even though the fashion changed. You could tell something about the wearer's rank and position in society by looking at:
- fabric textures
- colours and decorations (purple, then crimson, were the most important)
- jewellery
- headgear
- footwear.

From Han times, men wore loose robes with wide sleeves. Cloth was coloured with vegetable dyes. From Sui times, only emperors were allowed to wear yellow. Ordinary people had to dress in blue and black. White was the

hemp   a plant from which fibres are taken to make rope and cloth

colour for mourning and children could not wear white while their parents were alive. In AD 674 the government made strict laws to prevent people from hiding coloured clothing under their outer clothes.

During the Tang Dynasty, gold and silver rivalled **jade** and bronze in value. Chinese metalworkers were influenced by Persians who came to Chang'an. The Chinese adopted their ideas and began to beat metal into thin sheets and make objects from threads of metal.

1.5

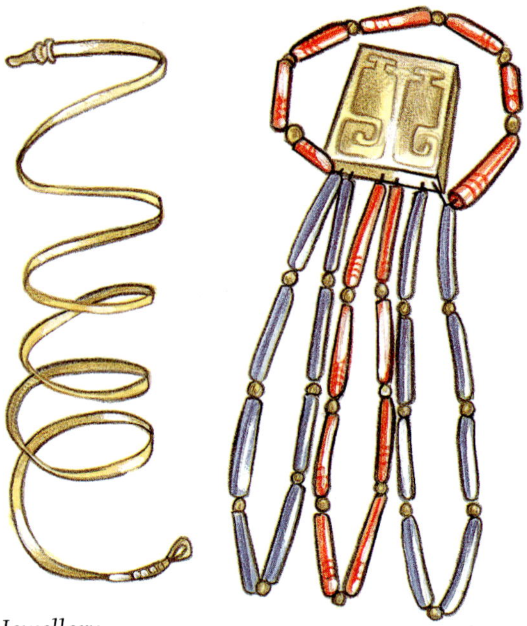

Jewellery

1.4

Clothing

The great cities

Chang'an

Chang'an, near the centre of modern Xian, was the capital of China during the time of the Western Han Dynasty. In the Han period it was the largest city in the world with a population of 500,000. The Northern and Southern Palaces were each 125 acres in size, and a tributary of the River Wei flowed past the Northern Palace. The city had a moat and drinking water came from the river. The Academy that trained students for official exams lay outside the walls. In AD 25 Chang'an ceased to be the capital, and the city was destroyed in AD 189.

In AD 589 under the Sui Dynasty (AD 581–618) a new Chang'an, south of the Han city became the Chinese capital. Emperor Wendi of the Sui Dynasty

jade   a semi-precious stone, usually green but sometimes white or blue

(AD 581–604) built his palace here. Li Yuan, who taking the name Gaozu became the first emperor of the Tang Dynasty, captured the city in AD 617. Under the Tang Dynasty (AD 618–906), Chang'an was at the centre of an empire. Its population increased to more than one million people, and the city itself grew to be 32 square miles in area, and had 100 merchant guilds and markets.

War at the end of the Tang Dynasty saw Chang'an destroyed and abandoned. The modern city on the site of the original palace dates from the Ming Dynasty.

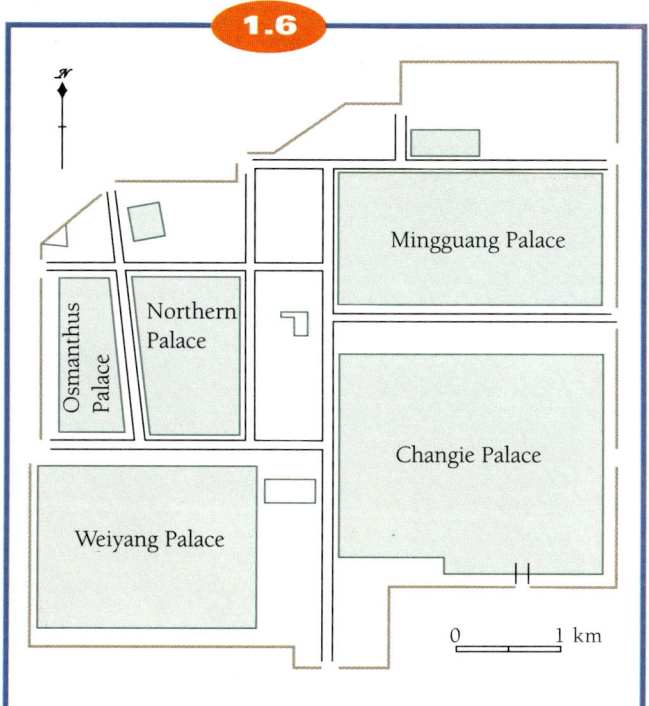

Chang'an during the Western Han period

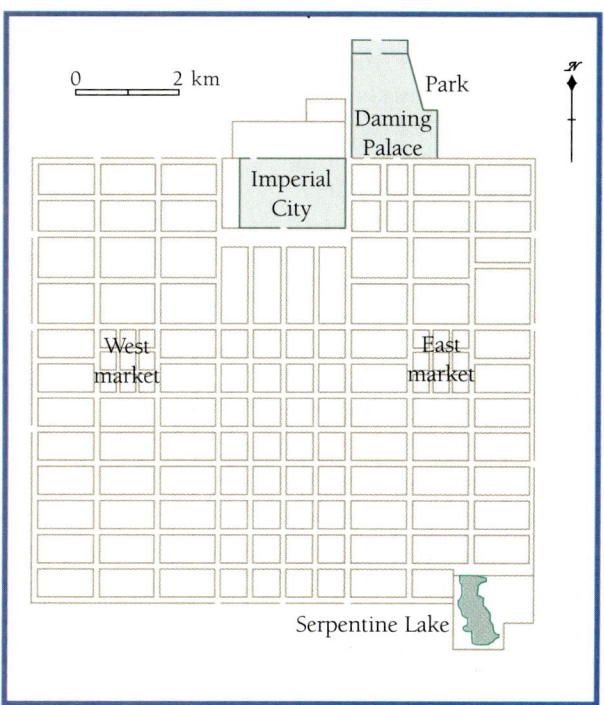

Chang'an during the Tang period

The great city of Chang'an

1.7

The great city of Chang'an had from generation to generation been the capital of all China. At this time it was Taizong of the dynasty of Tang who was on the throne. The whole land was at peace, tribute bearers poured in from every side and the whole world paid homage to him. One day, when he was receiving all his ministers at Court, the Prime Minister Wei Cheng submitted the following proposal: 'Now that the Empire is everywhere at peace, let us conform with the ancient custom and invite scholars from every quarter to come for examination, that your Majesty may have talent to assist you in your work of government.' The proposal was accepted, and a summons, sent all over China, inviting any that were learned in books, no matter whether they were soldiers or peasants to come to the Capital and attend an examination.

Wu Ch'engen in Monkey

Civil service examinations **1.8**

Using the information

1 Look closely at source 1.4. Write a paragraph about the features of ancient Chinese clothing.
2 What does source 1.8 tell you about the things that were considered important to good government during the Tang Dynasty.
3 Imagine you live in Chang'an and work in the civil service or that you make silk. Describe your daily activity (approximately 100 words).

Luoyang

The city of Luoyang is in the Mang Mountains in the north of China near the Lo River. The Emperor's palace and gardens, enclosed by a high painted wall, lay in the north of the city.

In AD 25 Luoyang became the capital of the Han Empire. The Silk Road departed from the west wall gate and the markets were near the main gates. Officials supervised trade and collected taxes. Peasants living near Luoyang grew wheat, beans, cabbages and other crops.

Luoyang was destroyed in AD 311 by the Xiongnu tribe from the north, but was rebuilt and became the capital for the Northern Wei Emperor Xiao Wendi in AD 494.

Using the information

1 Look at sources 1.6 and 1.9. What similarities are there between Chang'an and Luoyang?
2 Make your own models of Chinese houses or figures of boys and girls. Dress them in costume according to information provided and your own research.

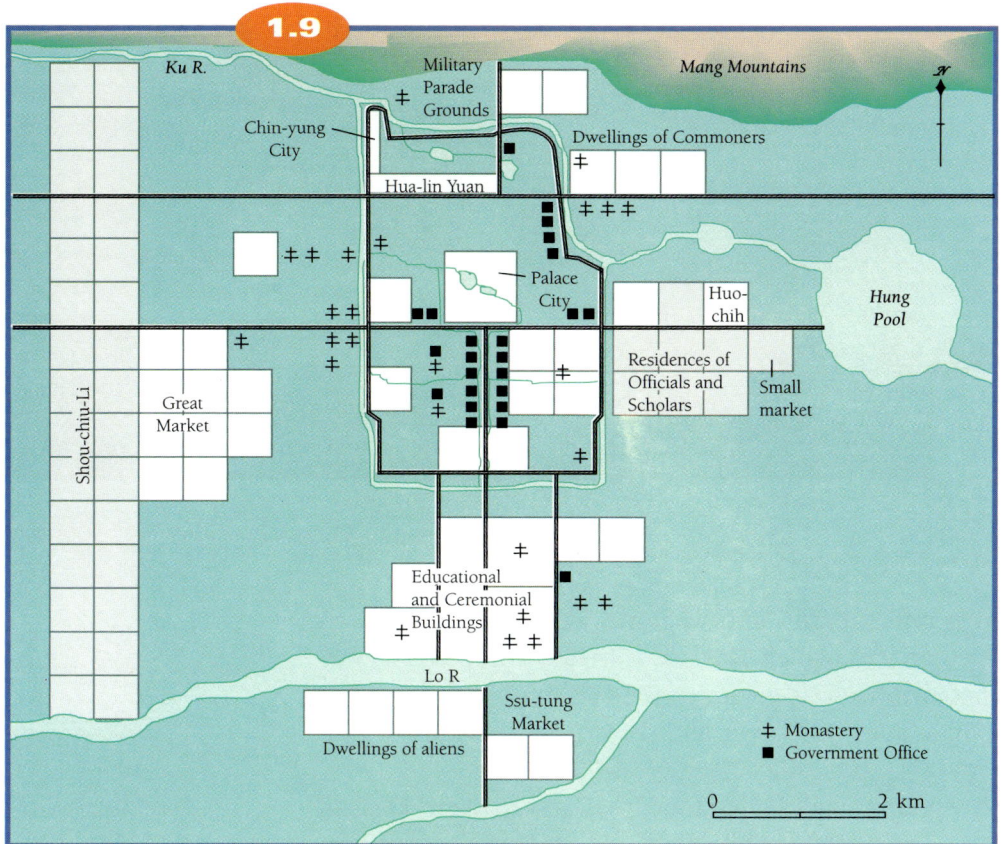

Luoyang

1.9

Ku R.

Military Parade Grounds

Mang Mountains

N

Chin-yung City

Dwellings of Commoners

Hua-lin Yuan

Palace City

Huo-chih

Hung Pool

Shou-chiu-Li

Great Market

Residences of Officials and Scholars

Small market

Educational and Ceremonial Buildings

Lo R

Ssu-tung Market

Dwellings of aliens

‡ Monastery
■ Government Office

0   2 km

Beijing

Beijing was the Capital of China under Kublai Khan and the Yuan Dynasty (AD 1260–1368). It was the capital again from the reign of Yongle during the Ming Dynasty.

From the outer city, a road led to the Forbidden City, which lay within the Imperial City (see source 1.10). The Ming empire was ruled from here.

The Forbidden City, 250 acres in size and in use for 500 years, was built in Beijing between AD 1406 and AD 1421 for Emperor Yongle. It had three main halls and two main temples. The Imperial City housed officials and the nobility, and everyone else lived in the Outer City. The main gateway was called the Gate of Heavenly Peace (Qianmen).

1.10

Tatar or Inner City

Imperial City

Forbidden City

Qianmen or Front Gate

Chinese or Outer City

Simplified plan of Imperial Beijing

1.11

Building a dyke

Using the information

Examine source 1.11. Identify what the people are doing and the tools they are using.

Farming

In early times, grains such as millet, barley and sorghum were grown in the north of the country rather than rice, which was not cultivated in the cool land of the Yellow River. In the south, rice was grown in the soft mud of the **paddy** fields, and fruit and vegetables, such as lychees and snow peas, were also grown.

Farmers worked with wooden spades and stone hoes and made terraces in the hill slopes to grow crops. This practice prevented **soil erosion**. Agriculture was often located close to the town and **night soil** was used as a fertiliser. The Chinese invented irrigation machines to raise the water from the canals and streams to irrigate the fields.

Peasants did not keep many large animals because they did not want to waste their land growing fodder for animals, but domesticated animals included cattle, pigs, chickens and other poultry.

In addition to working on the land, peasants also had to serve in the army and work building walls, canals and **dykes** under the corvee system.

Salt was produced from coastal areas and inland lakes.

The silkworm industry (sericulture)

Chinese legend tells how around 2700 BC insects were eating the Yellow Emperor's mulberry trees. He asked his wife to find out what they were and she found white worms eating the leaves and spinning cocoons. When she accidentally dropped one in hot water, a slender thread of silk began to unwind.

A cocoon spun by a Bombyx mori silkworm

1.12

paddy   a low lying field where rice is grown in water
soil erosion   loss of soil through water running downhill

collecting mulberry leaves

In China, wild silkworms or *tussah* feed on oak leaves, but cultivated silkworms are fed mulberry leaves. A female moth lays 300 to 500 eggs. When the silkworm is fully grown, it stops eating and spins a cocoon. To make silk, the cocoon is soaked in hot water, then spun, dyed and woven (see source 1.13). If the worm became a moth (approximately three weeks later) it would break the silk.

1.13   *Making silk*

feeding the silk worms

spinning silk

dyeing the silk

weaving the silk

Using the information

1   Draw a flow chart to show the different stages of making silk.
2   Find information on the Internet and in your local library on sericulture and give a short talk to the class on the subject. Try these web sites:
http://www.binary.net/silkery/invent.html
http://cecc-1.gnsu.ac.kr/~shinwha/silkhist.html

night soil   human excrement
dyke   a wall to prevent flooding

In this chapter, you will be investigating the following issues:
- How are fact and myths and legends related?
- What are the philosophies and religions of ancient China?
- Why is archaeological evidence a key to understanding ancient Chinese history?

Mythology

Chinese mythology explains that Pangu was the creator of the Universe, and eventually (after 18,000 years) different parts of his body became the sun, the moon, the rivers and seas, the trees and plants.

According to legend, the first four sovereigns who ruled China were:
- Fuxi, who invented the calendar, writing and musical instruments
- Shennong, the Red Emperor, who was the father of agriculture and who taught herbal medicine, set up markets and invented the plough
- Sui Ren, who discovered fire
- Huangdi, the Yellow Emperor, who founded the Chinese nation.

2.1

Gods: Fuxi, Shennong and Huangdi

The Ten Suns

2.2

It was the reign of Yao during the twenty-fourth century BC. The people were happy and contented because their emperor was wise and compassionate. Early in the morning the farmers ploughed the fields with the hope of good harvest, the hunters took their dogs to the forests with the expectation of bringing home their best catch and womenfolk carried pails of clothing to the riverside with a song on their lips. As these happy people carried out their routine jobs the sun slowly crept above the mountain peak, piercing the veil of clouds, bringing warmth and cheer to the hardworking people and filling their hearts with hopes and dreams.

Although the people felt and enjoyed the sun every day they knew little about the sun. They could not imagine that there were as many as ten suns. These suns were the children of the heavenly king and the sun goddess …

One day the youngest and the most mischievous of the suns came up with an idea.

The ten suns that rose above the misty mountain created an arc of fire scorching the earth, setting every combustible material on fire, drying every well and stream, making every living thing wither and threatening every life. The emperor fervently prayed to the heavenly king for help.

The heavenly king heard the fervent prayers and knew that he had to punish his sons. So he summoned his best archer, Hou Yi, and ordered him to do something to rescue the people on earth … One by one he shot his magic arrows. One by one the suns fell into the ocean until finally only one sun was left in the sky.

From Evelyn Lip, *Classic Chinese Legends*, Times, 1996.

Using the information

1 What can you find out about the period of the legendary emperors from the timeline inside the front cover?
2 Why is it difficult for historians to know what really happened so long ago?

Exploring the issues

1 What do you think the myth in source 2.2 is trying to explain?
2 How and why do you think a myth like this begins?
3 Do you think that myths like this can be useful to historians? Why?

The Chinese zodiac

The Chinese New Year begins, usually in February, at the time of the new moon. The Ancient Chinese divided the years into twelve-year cycles with each year represented by a different animal. People were thought to share certain characteristics of the animal that represented the year of their birth. Some Chinese still believe that the most auspicious, or lucky, year in which to be born is the Year of the Tiger. 1986 and 1998 were both Tiger years (see source 2.3).

Using the information

1 Look up your birth date and those of members of your family on the calendar in source 2.3. In the year of which animal were you born?
2 Using the Internet, or the library, find out about the characteristics of people born in those years. Try these web sites:
http://www.astro-fengshui.com/astrology.htm
http://www.chinese-astrology.com

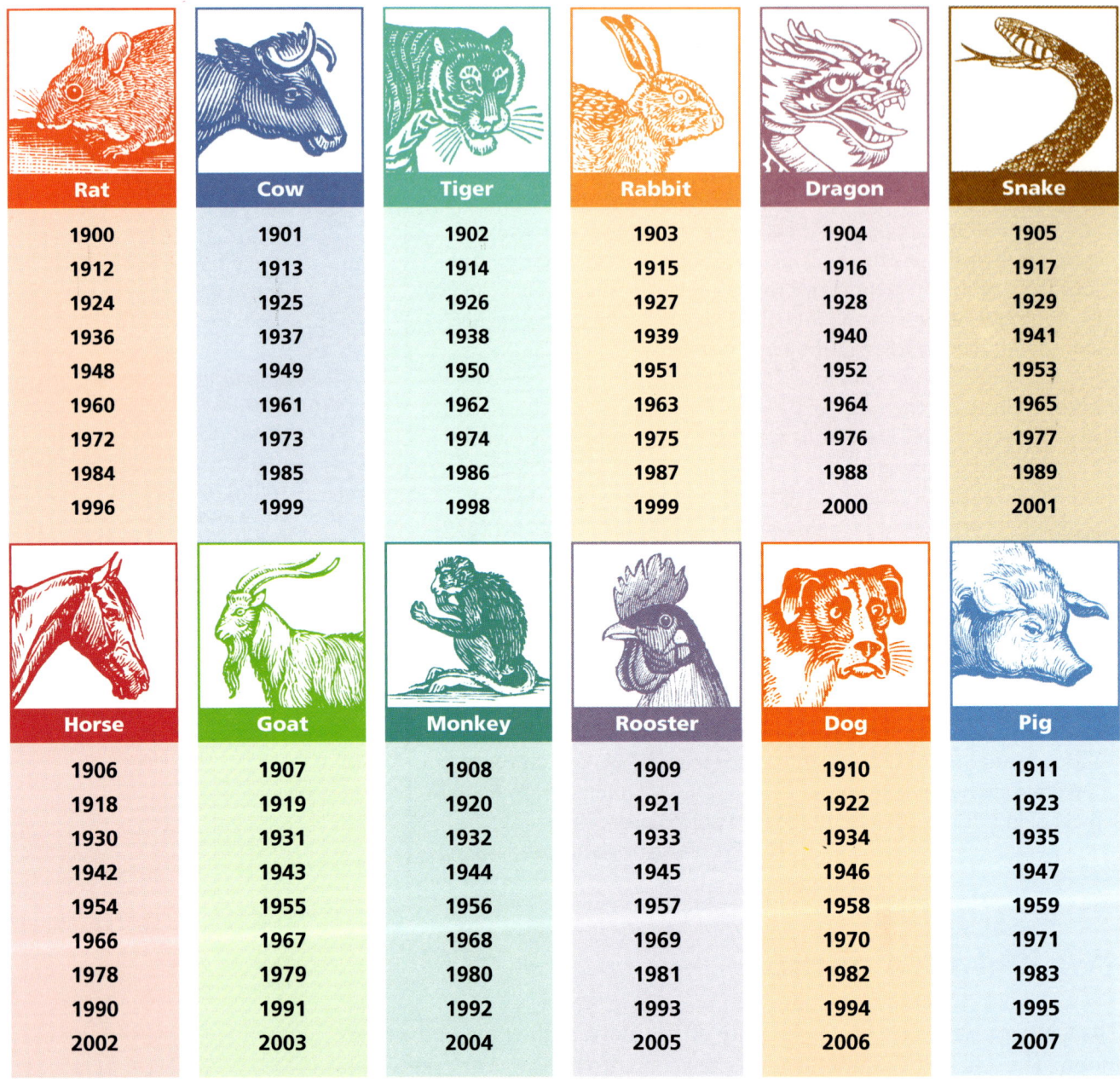

Rat	Cow	Tiger	Rabbit	Dragon	Snake
1900	1901	1902	1903	1904	1905
1912	1913	1914	1915	1916	1917
1924	1925	1926	1927	1928	1929
1936	1937	1938	1939	1940	1941
1948	1949	1950	1951	1952	1953
1960	1961	1962	1963	1964	1965
1972	1973	1974	1975	1976	1977
1984	1985	1986	1987	1988	1989
1996	1999	1998	1999	2000	2001

Horse	Goat	Monkey	Rooster	Dog	Pig
1906	1907	1908	1909	1910	1911
1918	1919	1920	1921	1922	1923
1930	1931	1932	1933	1934	1935
1942	1943	1944	1945	1946	1947
1954	1955	1956	1957	1958	1959
1966	1967	1968	1969	1970	1971
1978	1979	1980	1981	1982	1983
1990	1991	1992	1993	1994	1995
2002	2003	2004	2005	2006	2007

2.3 *Horoscope calendar*

Oracle bones

The Ancient Chinese believed that you could foretell the future by reading the cracks on an animal's shoulder bone (*scapula*) or a turtle shell (*plastra*) that had been heated over flames. The cracks were numbered and interpreted, and the prediction written on the bones by professional fortune tellers called diviners. The names of 120 diviners of oracle bones are known as a result of information obtained from these bones.

Oracle bones were used to ask questions about many things including military campaigns: for example, How many men should the king use and where should he send them?

Some pieces of tortoise shell and animal bones, found in the Yellow River Valley, can be dated back to 1751 BC. The discovery of oracle bones, which recorded events and the names of people, established that the Shang period was more than just a legend. Oracle bones have provided evidence of the last nine Shang kings in the period between 1200 and 1050 BC. People writing on oracle bones in the ancient past always dated them by recording the year of the reigning ruler. Another of the things we know from the bones is that in the Yin period of the Shang Dynasty, Anyang was the capital of China.

2.4

Shang oracle bone

Researching the past

1   What are scapula and plastra?
2   How were oracle bones used in ancient China and what is their importance for a historian today?

Using the information

Work in groups of three. One person writes a question for the diviner. Another is the diviner who writes an answer for the question. The third member of the group is a historian who makes a note of the useful information he or she can find out about daily life from both the question and the answer.

Philosophy and religious beliefs

The ancient Chinese and Chinese people today share three major beliefs: Confucianism, Daoism and Buddhism. Daoism and Buddhism are religions, but Confucianism is a philosophy.

Confucianism was established as the state ideology in 134 BC but Buddhism became the major religion in the Han Period (206 BC–220 AD).

Confucianism

Confucianism is based on the teachings of Confucius who lived from 551–479 BC. Confucius or Kongfuzi was born in Tsou. At the age of 19 he worked as a civil servant and began teaching when he was 22 years old.

Confucius believed that society is made up of those who rule and those who are ruled. He believed that we have duties and obligations to each other and that people should be disciplined. The most important duty is the child's duty to his or her parents, which he called filial piety. According to Confucius, children owe everything to their parents and must obey them completely for as long as they live, and honour and preserve their memory when they are dead. After his death, many of Confucius' teachings were put into a book called the *Analects*. In this book his teachings appear in question and answer form.

2.5

Confucius, Laozi and Buddha

2.6

Sayings of Confucius

- Confucius said: 'The superior person makes demands on himself; the inferior man makes demands on others.'
- Confucius said: 'The superior person seeks to enable people to succeed in what is good but does not help them in what is evil'.
- Confucius said: 'Lead the people by laws and regulate them by penalties, and the people will try to keep out of jail, but will have no sense of shame. Lead the people by virtue and restrain them by the rules of decorum, and the people will have a sense of shame, and moreover will become good.'
- The Duke of She asked about good government. Confucius said: 'A government is good when those near are happy and those far off are attracted.'

Using the information

Read source 2.6.
1   What is Confucius' attitude to making laws? How does he think people will be encouraged to keep the law?
2   What is his attitude to government?
3   List three things that Confucius taught.
4   Draw up a chart listing the different beliefs of Confucius, Laozi and Buddha.

Daoism

Laozi (c.604–531 BC), the founder of Daoism, preached the importance of kindness and love and warned against ambition. Laozi believed that people should lead a simple life focusing on meditation and the study of nature. In addition, he thought that there should not be too many regulations and that people should not be so interested in wealth.

Daoists worshipped 'immortals'. These immortals had magic powers and could become invisible, raise the dead and turn objects into gold. Daoism promised people immortality and Daoists believed in a hell. They also believed that there are a number of gods and a supreme god called *Hunlao*. Daoism looks at the relationship a person has with nature. The most important Daoist text is the *Dao de Jing* (*The Way and Power*) written by Laozi.

The Daoists taught 'the Way' but instead of emphasising 'duty', they preached 'harmony' and contacted the spirit world through magic. They were interested in science, herbal medicine and alchemy. The idea that the world is composed of opposites — the Yin and the Yang (the male and the female parts of nature) — is a Daoist idea.

2.7

Yin and Yang

Using the information

1   What is the Yin and the Yang?
2   What is 'the Way'?

2.8

The Way

The questioner said: If one follows the Way, one dies. If one does not follow the Way, one dies. What difference is there?

Mozi said: You are the sort of person who, having not a single day of goodness, yet seeks a lifetime of fame. If one has the Way, even if one dies, one's soul goes to an abode of happiness. If one does not have the Way, when he is dead one's soul suffers misfortune.

De Bary, *Death and Rebirth*, p. 276–77.

Buddhism

The Buddha, Prince Siddharta Gautama, was born in Nepal in India in 563 BC. He believed that people should meditate and would have many different lives (reincarnations). As a person dies, he or she passes from one incarnation to the next. The goal is to achieve 'nirvana' (or non-existence). In order to do this, people should follow the sacred rules and not drink, kill, steal or commit adultery. In the Buddhist faith, women were valued as highly as men.

Buddhism arrived with missionaries from India who travelled the Silk Road to China. In the early period, the local people adapted the images of Buddha to their own traditional beliefs, such as their belief in 'Immortals'. The first Buddhist settlement was at Luoyang.

In the fourth century (AD 300s) the non-Chinese Emperors of northern China adopted Buddhism as their official religion, but they adapted it. Traditionally, Buddhists believed that the family was not particularly important, but ancestor worship was very important in China and continued, in spite of the acceptance of other Buddhist ideas. The Wei Emperors built imperial shrines glorifying Buddha in the cliffs near Luoyang in the period AD 460-435.

The Tang Emperors also supported Buddhism and during the Tang Dynasty, in AD 645, a great Chinese monk called Xuanzang returned from his travels in India and Asia with new ideas about the Buddhist faith.

2.9

Xuanzang

What do you think?

Which belief system do you think these people would have followed and why:
- a young, powerful ruler
- an elderly person
- a person in a lowly position?

Using the information

1 Explain reincarnation.
2 In what ways did the Chinese adapt Indian Buddhism?
3 Imagine you are a teacher in China. Explain to your students the different Chinese religions, beliefs and philosophies.

Death and burial

Western Han tombs

Tombs were status symbols in the Western Han period and burials became very elaborate. Tombs were designed in the same way as dwellings and contained models of the people in the household. Royal tombs did not have large models of warriors, as in the time of the First Emperor, but miniature figures were buried in pits around the tomb.

- *Yangjiawan, Xiangyang:* A tomb dating from c.179–141 BC, found in AD 1965 at Yangjiawan in Xiangyang, contained 3,000 miniature **cavalry** soldiers in formation.
- *Liu Sheng:* The tomb of Liu Sheng, discovered in AD 1968 at Mancheng, is built as a real house with stables and a bathroom. The tomb is tunnelled in rock. In the tomb you can see funeral objects, horses and chariots. Prince Liu Sheng is wearing a jade suit. This was believed to protect the body from decay.

cavalry   soldiers mounted on horseback

2.10

Jade suit

- *Emperor Han Jing Di:* In AD 1990 the joint tomb of Emperor Han Jing Di and his wife Empress Wang was found south of Yangling when workers were building a highway from Xian. It has 24 pits and more than 40,000 clay figures, one-third life size, 'including soldiers expected to fight Jing Di's underworld battles' — Jing Di's 'terracotta army'. The soldiers are smiling, not serious like the terracotta warriors of the First Qin Emperor. When Jing Di's tomb was uncovered, archaeologists found *Mingqi* (miniature burial items) and bronze **artefacts** including coins, measuring cups for grain and three-sided arrowheads. There were also agricultural implements, weapons and grain stored in jars.

- *Lady Dai:* The **mummified** body of Lady Dai, found in AD 1971 by workers building a hospital at Mawangdi near Hunan, was wrapped in the earliest known Chinese painting yet discovered. The second-century BC tomb contained 46 rolls of colourful silk and cloth and lacquer objects. The silk (made at the height of the silk trade) included a beautiful silk banner carried at the funeral with pictures depicting heaven and hell and a picture of Lady Dai in the middle. She was dressed in silk cloaks. A post-mortem showed that she died of heart failure brought on by stomach problems (138 melon seeds were found in her stomach). There were plates of meat, fish and fruit, and containers of beef soup and wine in the tomb, and 162 wooden servant figures, including musicians with wooden instruments.

Using the information

Imagine you are visiting one of the Western Han tombs described above. Write a short report of what you see. Use the format of the tomb inspection report below.

Tomb inspection report

Site location:_____

Tomb of:_____

Age of tomb: _____

Objects found in the tomb: _____

_____

_____

Conclusions from evidence in the tomb: _____

_____

_____

artefact   an object made by humans
mummified   preserved by embalming and wrapping

In this chapter, you will be investigating the following issues:
- How did feudal systems become an Empire?
- What measures did the First Emperor implement?
- How did a woman establish herself as Emperor?

Chinese society

The Emperor was worshipped as a god and ruled with the Mandate of Heaven, which was thought to be given to him by the gods. He could lose this mandate if he did not rule well. He was considered to be the father of the people and was responsible for their wellbeing.

Beneath the Emperor, society was divided into the following classes:
- governors
- state officials, nobles, scholars (*shih*)
- gentry — wealthy landowners
- soldiers
- merchants (*shang*)
- artisans (*gong*)
- peasants farmers (*nong*)
- slaves (slavery was not a widespread practice).

Merchants and soldiers did not have a high status in society.

3.1

The moral power of the ruler

… King Ling loved slim waists and all the women went on diets and starved themselves. The King of Yüeh admired bravery and all the men outdid each other in dangerous feats defying death. From this we may see that he who wields authority can change the customs and transform the manners of his people.

From Huai-nan Tzu, 9:8b-9a, in Sources of Chinese Tradition, Vol 1.

Using the information

1 In what ways could a ruler influence the customs and traditions of his people?
2 What responsibilities did an Emperor have?
3 Draw a diagram or mind map of society with the Emperor at the top and the slaves at the bottom.

Qin Shihuangdi

Qin Shihuangdi was born in 259 BC at a time of feudal warring between seven states. He became King Zheng of Qin at 13 years old and improved the administration of his state and its agriculture. He was known as the Tiger of Qin. Qin Shihuangdi became the most powerful leader in China and in 221 BC declared himself Shihuangdi — The First August Emperor.

feudalism a system where an overlord gives people protection and land in return for services
axle a shaft on which wheels revolve

Qin Shihuangdi unified China. His capital, Xiangyang, was the centre of an empire that was linked by more than 7,500 kilometres of roads. Each province was ruled by a governor who collected the taxes. Qin Shihuangdi:

- abolished **feudalism**
- standardised the width of **axles** used on transport vehicles
- standardised weights and measures
- introduced a law code
- introduced a single **currency**
- introduced a single written language (script) simplifying what had been previously used
- conducted a census to count the population
- extended the Great Wall of China to more than 4,000 kilometres
- recognised private ownership of land.

Unfortunately, Qin Shihuangdi's rule became **authoritarian**. He ordered the 'Burning of the Books', which destroyed books that might be used to challenge his authority. He believed that people needed to be controlled by harsh laws (legalism). Qin Shihuangdi died in 210 BC.

The Qin empire

3.3

The Burning of the Books

Your servant suggests that all books in the imperial archives, except the memoirs of Qin be burned … Anyone referring to the past to criticise the present should, together with all members of his family, be put to death … Those who have not destroyed their books are to be sent to build the Great Wall.

Li Si

Using the information

1 Look carefully at source 3.2. Where is the capital, Xianyang, on the map?
2 What was the 'Burning of the Books' and why did it happen?

Han Wudi

Though not an active soldier himself, Han Wudi's 54-year reign (141–87 BC) saw the size of the Chinese empire double. The empire was divided into 83 provinces, then into prefectures, then into districts and then into wards. Centralised imperial rule was established. The empire was Jian Xia ('all under heaven'). Han Wudi was a follower of Confucius. During his long reign, he:

- controlled the size of the population
- encouraged agriculture and horse breeding
- established state monopolies on certain goods including iron, salt and alcohol
- had a canal built 128 kilometres (80 miles) long, linking the capital Chang'an to the Yellow River
- sent armies to the north, south and west and into Vietnam and Korea from 135 BC
- fought the Xiongnu
- founded an Imperial Academy to train officials
- sent Zhang Qian to make contact with other societies, and seek help from the Yuezhi people against the **nomadic** Xiongnu.

Han Wudi was educated and a good administrator. In his twenties he sent armies in search of conquests. His soldiers marched further than the greatest Roman legions and opened up the silk trade route as it moved 3,000 kilometres (1,864 miles) from home. Han Wudi left military settlements in Korea but his wars against the Xiongnu nomads, in the north, cost hundreds of thousands of lives.

The wars impoverished the economy. Merchants made money but there was a large class of poor people. Powerful families fought to see who would provide the next emperor. In 91 BC the Emperor's wife of almost 50 years, the Empress Wei and her family, were murdered by the Li family. Zhaodi, (the person chosen to rule, two days before Han Wudi died), was not related to either powerful group.

Writing about history

1 Look at source 3.4. Imagine you are Zhang Qian. Write a short report of one of your trips using details shown on the map.
2 Do you think Han Wudi was a good Emperor? Give your reasons based on the evidence of his reforms and his military conquests.

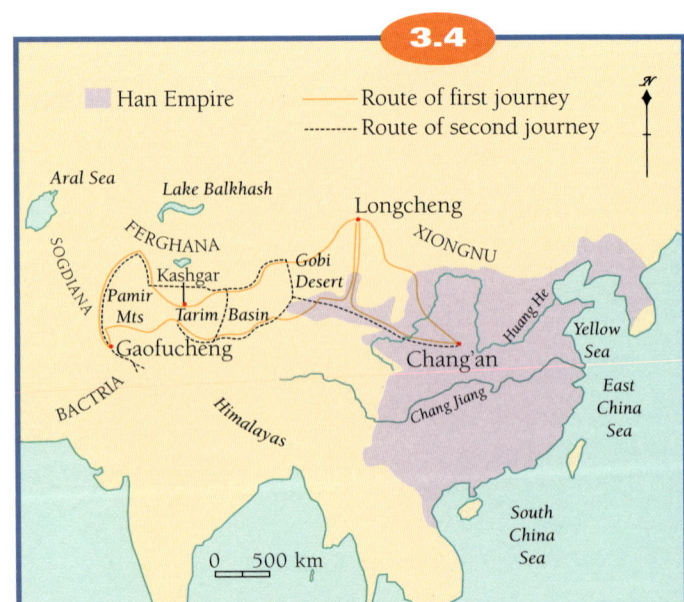

The Han empire

---

nomadic   moving from place to place in search of food, water, pasture or trade

Wu Zetian

3.5

Wu Zetian (originally called Wu Zhao) was a concubine of the Emperor Taizong and then consort to the next Emperor Gaozong during the Tang Dynasty. She was a ruthless person. She wanted power so she successfully accused the Emperor's wife, the Empress Wang of murder. She took over as Empress and principal wife of the Emperor Gaozong.

Emperor Gaozong was in power from AD 649–683. Wu Zetian was determined she would keep her power after he died. So:

- she had the Crown Prince poisoned
- exiled princes who were a threat
- persuaded Gaozong to nominate her son, Li Zhe, as heir
- obtained support from the Buddhist church by funding Buddhist art and architecture
- promoted the idea that a woman could be Emperor
- butchered the former Empress Wang, chopping off her arms and legs
- killed or exiled opponents
- operated a ruthless secret service
- took the title 'Heavenly Empress'.

When Gaozong died, Wu Zetian was the person who was really in charge. Six years later she forced the Emperor Ruizong to abdicate and she became the first and only female Emperor of China.

Empress Wu was a Buddhist and ruled from AD 690–705 expanding China's foreign policy and promoting the idea that she was a god. She portrayed herself as a female Buddha, 'Maitreya the Peerless'.

Wu Zetian

What do you think?

Imagine you are Empress Wu. What is your most important claim to fame? Prepare a speech to your subjects celebrating your achievements (approximately 150 words).

Genghis Khan

Genghis Khan was the leader, the Khagan, of the Mongol peoples to the north of China. They were **marauding** horse riders, skilled in the art of war, who lived a nomadic life on the plains. The Chinese had sought to keep them out of China by building the Great Wall. However, the Mongol peoples invaded China.

Genghis Khan was born in AD 1162 in Mongolia and named Temujin, which means 'blacksmith'. As a boy, Temujin was told by his religious adviser (shaman) that Tingri, the Mongol supreme god, had chosen him to be ruler of the world.

marauding   attacking, raiding

The Mongol text, *The Secret History of Genghis Khan*, says that Temujin's father was poisoned when the boy was nine years old. Temujin's two close friends were Jamuga (a **blood brother**) and Toghri. However, later they opposed his growing power and in AD 1205 Temujin put his blood brother to death. In AD 1206 at the age of 40, Temujin became Genghis Khan at a great assembly called a 'kuriltai'. Genghis Khan is a title meaning 'strong ruler' or 'universal ruler'. His capital was Karakorum.

Crossing the Gobi desert in his first campaign in AD 1209 with **Bactrian camels**, Genghis Khan travelled across the Guruan Sayhan Mountains and into the kingdom of Xi Xia and then attacked the Jin empire in the north of China in AD 1211 with an army of 70,000 and conquered Beijing in AD 1215. However, he died in AD 1227 before he could conquer all China.

3.6

Genghis Khan praying to the sun before going into battle

Using the information

1 What countries formed the Mongol empire in AD 1224?
2 What characteristics of Genghis Khan made him a successful leader?

blood brother   sealing a bond between two people by mixing blood
Bactrian camel   a camel with two humps, used to transport goods along the Silk Road

The Mongol Empire in AD 1294 showing the routes of Ghengis Khan's campaigns

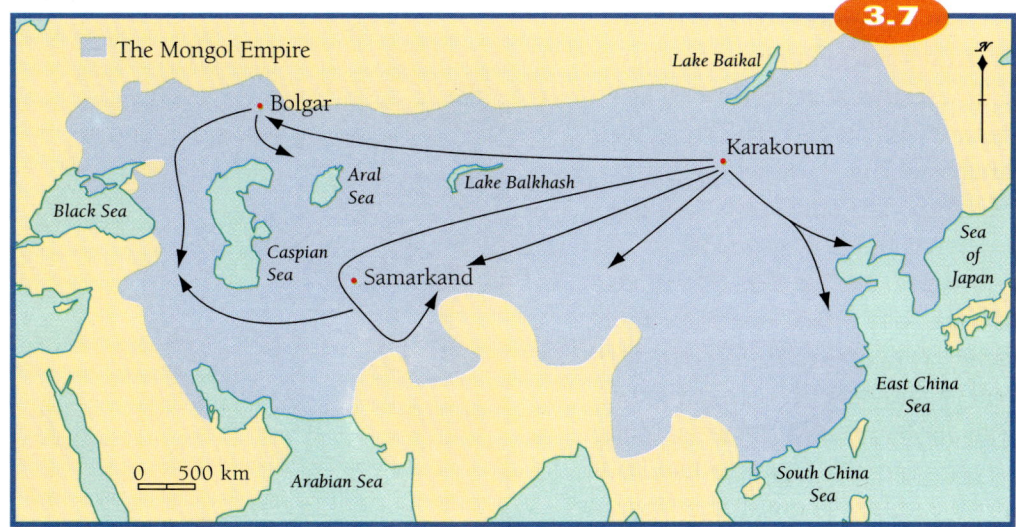

Kublai Khan (Yuan Dynasty)

Kublai Khan was born in AD 1215. His mother was a Nestorian Christian and believed people should have religious freedom. She made sure her son could read and write.

The Mongols had controlled northern China since AD 1234. Used to fighting on dry land, they found the rivers and canals, mountains and forests in the south of China more difficult.

In AD 1253 Kublai Khan fought successfully in the south and when his brother Mongke Khan died in AD 1259, he resisted the opposition of his younger brother Arigh Boke and declared himself Great Khan in AD 1260.

Kublai Khan moved his capital to the city of Beijing in the south and from AD 1271 called himself Emperor of China, founding the Yuan Dynasty. The Chinese Song Dynasty in the south was finally defeated in AD 1279. Kublai Khan allowed the Chinese to rule themselves with Mongol supervision. The population was divided into four classes: Mongols, non-Chinese, northern Chinese and, last and least, southern Chinese.

Kublai Khan:

*   encouraged trade
*   used paper money with Chinese and Mongolian writing
*   joined the Yellow River and Dadu (Beijing) by extending the Grand Canal
*   extended the postal service (a horse and rider would travel 400 kilometres a day stopping for fresh horses)
*   encouraged religious freedom.

Like other Mongol leaders, Kublai Khan had four main wives but his favourite wife was a Buddhist woman called Chabi. She was intelligent and literate, and like her husband, believed in working peacefully with the Chinese people.

In 1268 AD Kublai Khan conquered northern China and Korea. During the reign of Kublai Khan, two disasters ruined his hopes of an overseas empire. He sent two fleets against the Japanese but both met adverse conditions at sea and were damaged by storms.

In November AD 1274, 900 ships with 40,000 men (Mongol, Chinese and Korean) landed at Japan's Hakata Bay. The ships were anchored but that night a storm blew up. The ships sailed for the open sea but 200 were lost.

In AD 1281 a fleet five times the size of the first one with three times as many troops prepared to sail. Again, the Chinese landed at Hakata Bay, but in the intervening seven years the Japanese had built fortifications. The wall the Japanese had constructed stopped the Mongols from using their famous cavalry charge. Over the weeks the fighting was equal. More Chinese troops arrived two months later and by August the Chinese were preparing to attack the mainland at Kyushu but once again a storm struck, destroying the fleet. Kublai Khan died in AD 1294.

Kublai Khan laying siege to a Chinese fortress

Using the information

1   Imagine you are Emperor Kublai Khan. You have just had word that your fleet has been destroyed by a storm. Prepare a speech to your subjects (approximately 150 words).

2   Search the Internet and download more information on Kublai Khan and his achievements. Present the information either in the form of a poster or as a short talk to your class. Try these web sites:
     http://m1.aol.com/oyunbilig.fame.htm
     http://members.tripod.com/boroo/ChronologicalTable.html
     http://www.ccds.charlotte.nc.us/~nwhist/china/jaben/jaben.htm

In this chapter, you will be investigating the following issues:
* the importance of ancestor worship
* the role of sons and daughters in family life
* attitudes to education and marriage for boys and girls.

Ancestors

The Chinese believed that wisdom came with increasing age and elderly people were treated with great respect. When a person's parent died, mourning might last for up to three years.

The Chinese practised ancestor worship. They believed that their ancestors' spirits could protect the family. In most households there was an altar at which offerings were made to the dead. In the Han period the Confucian emphasis on filial piety, or respect for one's ancestors, saw an increased interest in tomb building as a way of honouring ancestors. People believed that life continued after death and that they would have the same needs in the afterlife that they had on Earth. For this reason household and personal objects were buried with the dead.

4.1 *Gentleman*

Children

Emperors and rich men had concubines or secondary wives. The children of these secondary wives had legal rights and were allowed to inherit property from their fathers.

The birth of a young male was considered more important than the birth of a girl for a number of reasons. A son would always carry the family name and live within the family home, whereas a daughter would marry and take the name of her husband. Also a dowry, consisting of money, clothes and household necessities, had to be provided for a daughter in order that she could marry. Furthermore, if the family worked on the land, a boy was seen as an extra pair of hands, whereas a daughter was another mouth to feed.

4.2 *Farmer*

When a boy was six or seven years old, he went to school or to work, perhaps as an apprentice or to work on a farm. If a family was poor, they might sell their children to work as servants. Richer families sent their children to be educated between the ages of seven and thirteen, or had them taught at home by tutors. Most religious training was done at home.

Women

Educating girls was not seen as important or necessary and girls learned household skills from their mothers. They were not given as much training in ancestor rituals as boys because when they married they had to transfer their respect and loyalty to their husband and his family. At the age of six or seven, many girls had their toes bound under the soles of their feet. Binding girls' toes was an accepted practice in the Song period. It produced horribly deformed feet, which were considered a status symbol. It showed that the family was so wealthy that the woman did not need to work. It was not a practice generally accepted by peasants.

A parent, possibly with the aid of a matchmaker, would arrange a child's marriage and **astrological** charts, drawn up at the time of their birth, would be an important factor in deciding whether the couple were well-matched. In a family, the young bride was virtually the servant of her mother-in-law and it was only the birth of her first son that gave a woman any status. The practice of men taking a concubine if their first wife did not give birth to a son also kept women's status inferior. A woman was not expected to remarry if her husband died.

Using the information

1 Explain in your own words the meaning of 'filial piety'.
2 Look at sources 4.1–4.4. What is each person doing? How are they dressed? Which class in society do they represent?

Exploring the issues

How does the fact that girls were not educated make it difficult for historians?

Writing about history

Imagine that you are the son of a rich family, and can therefore read and write. Consider how fortunate you are, both as a son and as a member of a rich family. Write approximately 150 words about your life. Consider such issues as filial piety, ancestor worship and your attitude to women.

4.3 *Artisan*

4.4 *Servant*

astrological relating to the study of the influence of the planets and stars on people's lives
fortress a fortified building

The military

In this chapter, you will be investigating the following issues:
- the need to fortify China's boundaries
- the structure and strategies of the Chinese army.

The Great Wall

The First Emperor of China reformed and reorganised his empire.

In 214 BC Qin Shihunagdi ordered his general Meng Jian to join the existing parts of the Great Wall (the Wall of the Ten Thousand Li). His job was to create **fortresses** on the western and northern borders of the Empire and protect the northern borders against attackers from the Gobi desert in central Asia.

5.1

The walls and towers of the Great Wall

The wall was sometimes built in the traditional Chinese way using rammed earth. Layer upon layer of earth pressed between wooden planks were separated by bamboo. The sides of the wall were faced and sealed with burnt bricks or plaster. Conditions in the Gobi desert required that the section of the Wall there was built of layers of sand, pebbles and twigs.

In some parts the wall was as much as 14 metres high; in others only 7 metres. But it was wide enough for five horses, riding side by side, to pass along the top of the **ramparts**. There were watchtowers on the walls. Signals could pass from the watchtowers to the main forts. Openings in the wall allowed crossbows to be fired.

rampart   a mound or wall protecting a building
barbarian   an uncivilised person — the Chinese believed that anyone who was not Chinese was uncivilised

The Wall:
- closed the gap between the Himalayas (and the plateaus of Yunnan and Tibet in the south) and the sea in the north
- was a defence against nomads
- defined the separation of the civilised 'Middle Kingdom' from the **barbarians**.

Source 5.3 is an account of how Xuanzang, the Buddhist monk who travelled to India in search of the Tripitaka, first saw the Great Wall.

5.2

The Master of the Law

Having pushed on eighty li or so, he saw the first watch-tower (Chinese frontier post). Fearing lest the lookouts should see him, he concealed himself in a hollow of sand until night; then going on west of the tower, he saw the water; and going down, he drank and washed his hands. Then as he was filling his water vessel with water an arrow whistled past him and just grazed his knee, and in a moment another arrow. Knowing then that he was discovered, he cried with a loud voice, 'I am a priest come from the capital; do not shoot me!' Then he led his horse towards the tower, whilst the men on guard opening the gate came out.

Biography of Xuanzang by Hwuilih.

Using the information

1. Why was the Great Wall of China built?
2. What was the purpose of a watchtower?

The terracotta warriors

Seven hundred thousand conscripted workers worked for 36 years to complete the tomb of Qin Shihuangdi (see source 5.3). The Chinese historian Sima Qian described this tomb as recreating and representing the **cosmos**. Today, we know it as the place where the famous terracotta army was found. The burial was preserved (though the roof had partly fallen in) when the pits were set alight by rebels some years after the Emperor's death. The fire baked the surface above the pits.

This buried army symbolised the Empire of the Qin Dynasty. The figures are more than life-size and show every detail of the weapons, armour, clothing and cultural origins and nationalities of the soldiers. (see sources 5.4 to 5.6).

Almost 10,000 terracotta figures were found during 1974 and in succeeding years in three pits east of the Emperor's tomb. The first pit contained 6,000 infantry and some **chariots** and horses. The second contained 1,400 soldiers, archers and cavalry. Sixty-eight senior officers were found in the third, which symbolised the army headquarters. The soldiers did not have shields but drums and gongs to create a noise. A fourth pit at Xian was unfinished at the time of Qin Shihuangdi's death.

Two moulds were made of the model soldiers (back and front), with limbs in assorted positions made separately. Clothes were sculptured and painted on

cosmos   the ordered universe
chariot   a two-wheeled horse-drawn vehicle

the models. Clay of highest quality was placed over the model and the features (hair, eyes, etc.) outlined. Other moulded parts were added (for example, the nose, armour) and then everything was fired in a kiln and later painted. The horses were made in two sections, left and right side. The wooden part of the archers' crossbows rotted over time.

5.3

The First Emperor's tomb

… the First Emperor was interred at Mt Li. When the emperor first came to the throne he began digging and shaping Mt Li. Later when he unified the empire, he had over 700,000 men from all over the empire transported to the spot. They dug down to the third layer of the underground springs and poured bronze to make the outer coffin. Replicas of palaces, scenic towers, and the hundred officials, as well as rare utensils and wonderful objects were brought to fill up the tomb. Craftsmen were ordered to set up crossbows and arrows, rigged so they would immediately shoot down anyone attempting to break in. Mercury was used to fashion imitations of the hundred rivers, the Yellow River and the Yangtze, and the seas, constructed in such a way that they seemed to flow. Above were representations of all the heavenly bodies, below the features of the earth. 'Man-fish' (possibly whale) oil was used for lamps, which were calculated to burn for a long time without going out.

Sima Qian, *Records of the Grand Historian: Qin Dynasty*, translated by Burton Watson, Columbia University Press, 1993.

5.4

Two warriors of Qin Shihuangdi's terracotta army

The commander-in-chief of the army has not been found. The reason for this is probably because the position of commander-in-chief was taken by the Emperor who could not be depicted because of his godlike status.

Faces of terracotta warriors

Rows of warriors

Writing about history

1 Imagine that you have arrived in Shanxi province to visit the tomb of Qin Shihuangdi. A kilometre from the tomb are the terracotta warriors, buried thousands of years ago. The Emperor was buried south of the hill (tumulus). As you walk into the first pit, you see the magnificent soldiers standing in rows flanked, by crossbowmen guarding the sides of the army. At the front of each row are chariots. Write a short diary entry expressing your feelings about this experience.

2 No face is alike. Look at the faces of the soldiers in source 5.5. Describe what you see in the picture.

3 Look at the terracotta warriors in sources 5.4, 5.5 and 5.6. Fill in the identity profile below.

4 What do sources 5.3 to 5.6 tell us about the society at the time?

5 Use the Internet to search for more information on the terracotta warriors. Try these web sites:
http://chinavista.com/travel/terracotta/main.html
http://www.mc.maricopa.edu/academic/cult•sci/anthro/asb-china/qin/terracotta2.html
http://members.aol.com/h2oskineil/travel/page10c.htm

Identity profile

*   Are they wearing headgear? Describe it.
*   What sort of clothing are they wearing?
*   What is the position of the hands and feet?
*   Are they wearing armour? Describe it.
*   What do you think their role may have been? What evidence supports your answer?

Writing about history

In your book fill out the tomb's inspection report using the format at right.

Tomb inspection report

Site location:_____

Tomb of:_____

Age of tomb:_____

Objects found in the tomb:_____

_____

Conclusions from evidence in the tomb:_____

_____

Weapons and warfare

Battle was mostly between foot soldiers, though cavalry were used. The cavalry rode Mongolian ponies and later the horses imported from **Ferghana** on the Silk Road. Swords, knives and axes were used in hand-to-hand combat.

Ferghana   modern Turkestan

A chariot carried an archer, the charioteer and a halberdier to protect the horses. A halberd was a dagger-shaped, bronze blade usually attached to a long bamboo pole, which the halberdier used like a scythe. The chariot ceased to be important by the Qin period because the crossbow made the chariot less effective. Before an **infantry** charge, a round of arrows was fired at the enemy ranks. The arrows from crossbows could pierce armour. They had a range of about 200 metres.

The formations of the terracotta warriors show foot soldiers in nine rows with four men in each row. There are archers in front and chariots behind the soldiers.

Sun Zi, author of *The Art of War*, written during the Zhou period, described the noise of battle: 'Now gongs and drums, banners and flags make the soldiers pay attention'.

Qin Shihuangdi did not have a professional army. Later dynasties had a paid armed force. As well as using poison arrows, in the Song and Yuan periods, the Chinese army used flame throwers and bombs. In approximately AD 1150 the Chinese developed the idea of putting gunpowder on the shaft of an arrow. With an iron weight attached to the arrow the 'rocket' could fly up to 335 metres (1,100 feet).

The soldiers had bamboo or wooden 'rocket launchers'. During a battle the Chinese could fire many thousands of rockets (up to 320 at a time). Bombs were also designed by enclosing explosives in wood, porcelain or metal containers.

5.7 *Rocket launcher*

Using the information

Imagine you are watching an army march through your Chinese village in medieval times. Describe what you can see.

infantry	foot soldiers
camel caravan	a number of camels used to transport goods

Trade

In this chapter, you will be investigating the following issues:
- How did the Silk Road become important in Chinese life?
- What improvements were made in communication?
- Why were the Chinese such an industrious and inventive people?

The Silk Road

The Chinese were called 'the *seres*' meaning 'the silk people'. The first Chinese merchants set out for Central Asia in 114 BC and their route became known as the Silk Road. The main Silk Road led from Chang'an to Central Asia. Other roads went south and then by sea through Indonesia to the Indian Ocean. The Silk Road went to Palmyra in Syria and then to ports in Tyre and Antioch. From there, goods went to Alexandria in Egypt. Bactria and its capital Balkh were on the Silk Road. Travellers on the route experienced both burning deserts and freezing snow.

In the time of the Han Dynasty, Chinese **camel caravans** stopped at Kashgar in central Asia. The goods would go from there to places such as Rome. Chinese exports included silk, rhubarb, lacquer ware, tea, cinnamon and other spices.

Goods imported into China included **pomegranates**, grapes, jade, pearls, linen, wood, **alfalfa**, gold, silver, furs, woollen material from Asia, glassware from Rome, and horses because it was difficult to breed horses in northern China.

The Silk Road brought Buddhism to China. However, it began to lose importance in the seventh century (AD 600s) as sea trade developed. It was generally safer to travel by sea as there was less chance of being attacked.

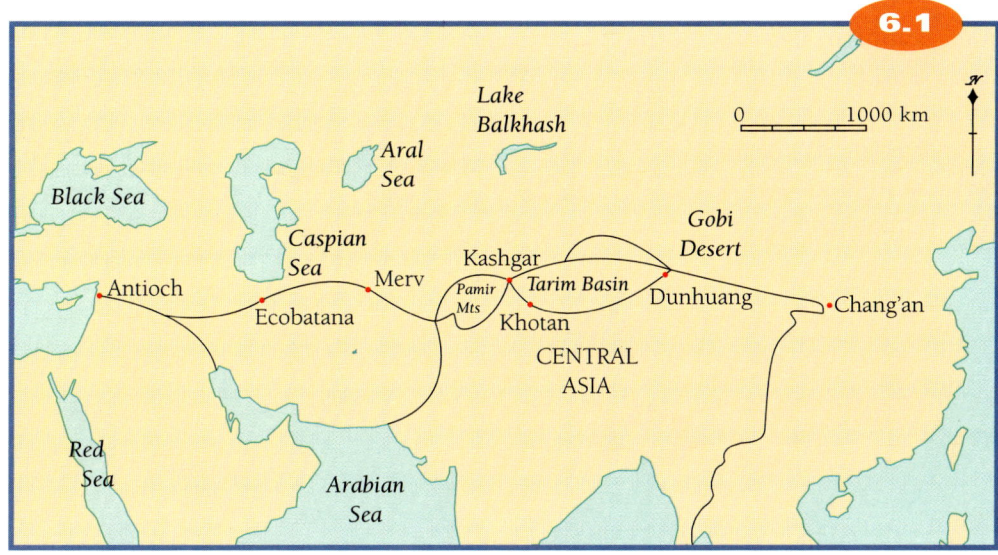

6.1

Silk Road trading routes

---

pomegranate a fruit containing many seeds
alfalfa a plant commonly fed to animals

The Silk Road in the Gobi Desert

6.2

Canals

Canals were built to improve transport and trade between cities. Emperor Wendi built canals but his successor Yangdi (emperor from AD 604–617) built a much larger canal system — the Grand Canal. It linked Beijing in the north with the city of Hangzhou in the south. Two thousand kilometres of canals linked the whole country except the province of Sichuan, providing transport for people and goods. It took more than five million people to build the canal system.

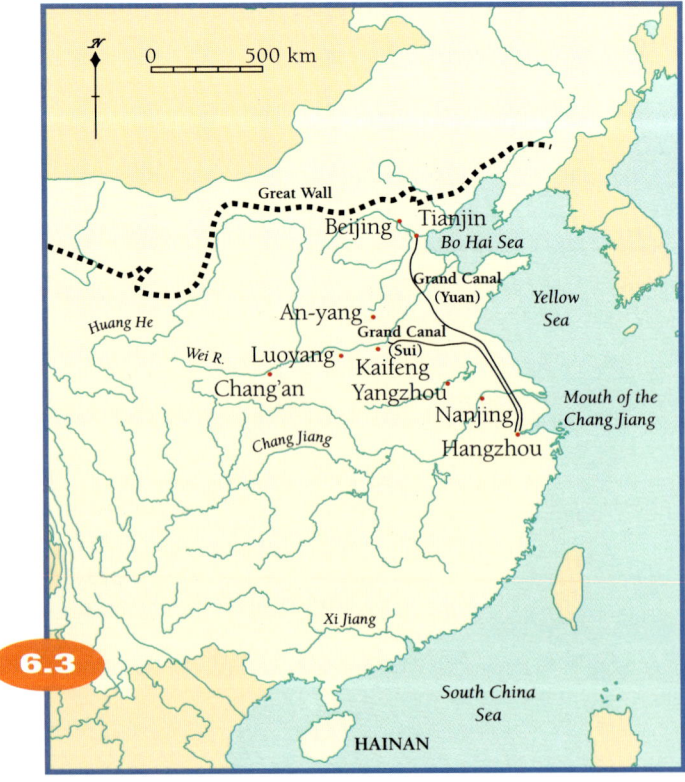

6.3

The Grand Canal

Horses

Zhang Qian was a famous traveller who brought news of the fast horses of Ferghana when he returned to China in 123 BC in the reign of the Han Emperor Wudi. These horses could cover 400 kilometres a day.

6.4

Ferghana horse

Marco Polo

Marco Polo was born in Venice in AD 1254 and died in AD 1324. In AD 1271 when he was 17 years old, he travelled with his father Nicolo, and his uncle Maffeo to China (it was then known as Cathay).

Arriving in AD 1275, Marco stayed in China in the service of the Chinese Emperor Kublai Khan for seventeen years and in that time he served for three years as a Governor in the city of Yangzhou and then later as Commissioner in the Emperor's Imperial Council. When the Emperor was in his seventies, the Polos decided it was time to go home because they feared they would not be safe with his successors.

Marco Polo reported that Kublai Khan had a postal service with relay stations every 40 kilometres. He also recorded that weak-sighted people in the court of Kublai Khan wore spectacles and it is from Marco Polo that we know that the Chinese used paper money.

When the Polos left to return home, Kublai Khan gave them a golden tablet that contained his orders for their safe conduct through China. He also

6.5

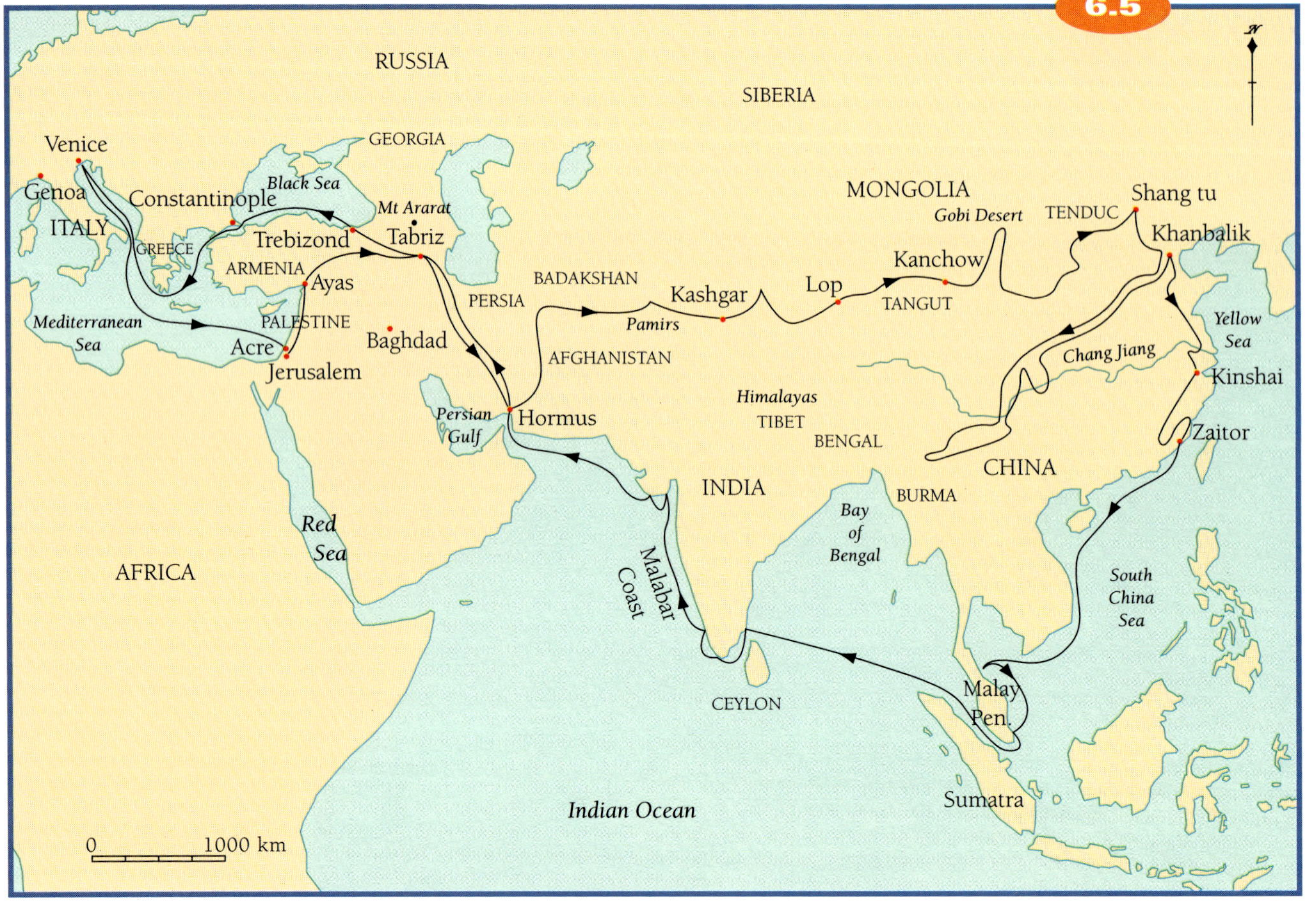

Marco Polo's travels

gave them supplies for themselves and their attendants. When they were back in Europe, they had Kublai Khan's authority to act as his ambassadors to the Pope, and the kings and princes of Europe. They reached home in AD 1295.

6.6

Marco Polo

6.7

Marco Polo's travels

Being introduced to the presence of the Grand Khan, Kublai, the travellers were received by him with ... affability ... and as they were the first Latins who had made their appearance in that country they were entertained with feasts and honoured with other marks of distinction. Entering graciously into conversation with them, he made earnest inquiries on the subject of the western parts of the world, of the Emperor of the Romans, and of other Christian kings and princes.

Marco Polo.

Ships

The Chinese traded with India in boats called junks in the ninth century (AD 800s).

Zheng He was a Chinese Muslim born in AD 1371. He was appointed commander of the Ming Dynasty fleet by Emperor Yongle. From AD 1405 Admiral Zheng He led seven successful naval expeditions. The first three went to Vietnam and as far as India. The next three, from AD 1413 to AD 1422, went as far as Somalia and Aden and the last, from AD 1431 to AD 1433, saw the Chinese set sail from the Ming capital Nanking and reach Mecca.

In his travels, Zheng He traded goods such as gold, porcelain, silk and spices. He also collected tribute from countries controlled by China. Zheng He died in AD 1433 after he returned from his seventh expedition.

Using the information

1   Imagine that you are Marco Polo. Write a letter about your experiences in China to your relatives back home.
2   What sort of person is Kublai Khan? What evidence is there in the sources to support your view?
3   Compare transport today with transport in medieval China. What are the similarities and differences?

6.8

Chinese junk

6.9

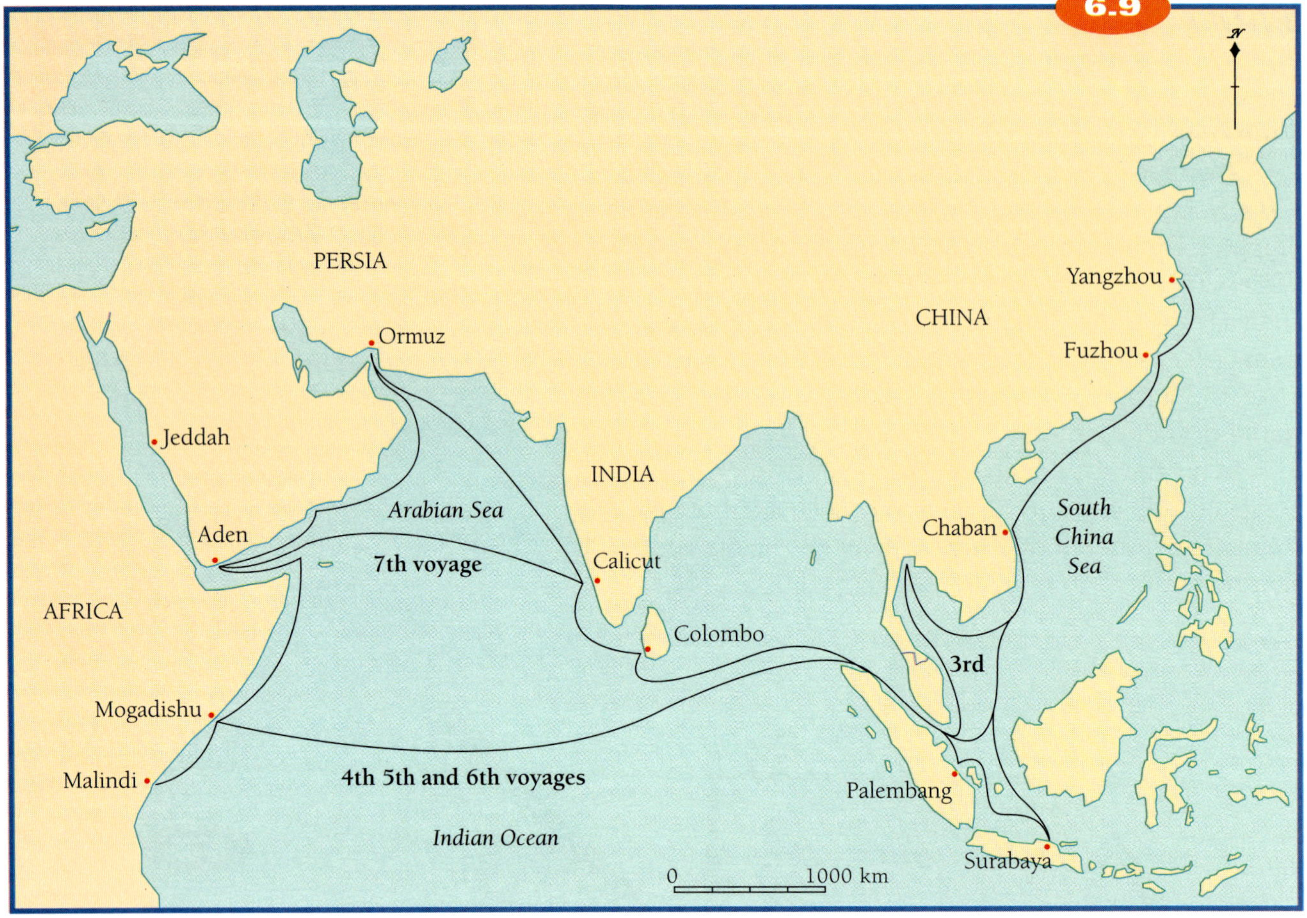

The map shows the expeditions of Zheng He, with labelled locations including PERSIA, Ormuz, Jeddah, Aden, AFRICA, Mogadishu, Malindi, Arabian Sea, INDIA, Calicut, Colombo, CHINA, Yangzhou, Fuzhou, Chaban, South China Sea, Palembang, Surabaya, Indian Ocean. Routes are labelled "7th voyage", "4th 5th and 6th voyages", and "3rd".

0 — 1000 km

The expeditions of Zheng He

What do you think?

What qualities would a successful admiral need to command a voyage of exploration?

Using the information

1 Draw up a timeline of Zheng He's travels.
2 Construct a model of a Chinese junk, based on the illustration.
3 Imagine travelling with Zheng He on his voyages. Describe what you think life on a junk would be like (approximately 150 words).

Researching the past

What is tribute?

Exploring the issues

What does the appointment of a Muslim fleet commander indicate about the Emperor's attitude?

| elite | the most powerful, gifted or wealthy group in a community | vertically horizontally | going straight up and down level with the horizon |

Arts and sciences

7

In this chapter, you will be investigating the following issues:
*   How did Chinese writing develop?
*   What practical needs influenced Chinese arts and sciences?
*   What contribution did Chinese discoveries and invention make to our modern world?

Writing

7.1

Until AD 2000, picture writing was thought to have developed during the Shang Dynasty. Recent discoveries suggest an even earlier development. Chinese pictograms did not evolve in the way they did in Egypt. They did not come to reflect a sound so the Chinese needed thousands of pictograms to convey ideas and concepts. There are about 50,000 characters in the Chinese alphabet. Writing was restricted to the **elite** who could afford an education.

Before paper was invented the Chinese wrote on bamboo. They cut the characters into the wood in thin strips, writing from top to bottom. All Chinese writing is read **vertically** not **horizontally**. The earliest complete printed book is *The Diamond Sutra*, which was printed in AD 868.

The practice developed of painting on material, especially on silk. Some individual characters have up to 26 brush strokes that must be put down in the correct order.

Paper was invented by Cailun in AD 105. He was a **eunuch** in the court of Emperor Ho-ti. When the Chinese invaded Samarkand in AD 751, they were defeated. Captured Chinese papermakers gave the secret of papermaking to their Arab conquerors.

Printing began in China about AD 165 when ink rubbings were made on text cut in stone.

A process for making paper

1	Cut hemp.
2	Mix with water.
3	Tread.
4	Make **potash**.
5	Mix with water.
6	Strain.
7	Steam ash and hemp paste.
8	Pulp.
9	Wash in water.
10	Spread pulp on gauze frames.
11	Dry in sun.

7.2

Paper making

In ancient times writing was generally on bamboo or on pieces of silk, which was then called 'Chich'. But the silk being expensive and bamboo heavy these two materials were not convenient. Then Cailun thought of using tree bark, hemp, rags and fish nets. In the first year of the Yuan Hsing period (AD 105) he made a report on the process of paper making and received high praise for his ability. From this time paper has been in use everywhere.

Tan Yeh in *The Macquarie History of Ideas*, The Macquarie Library, 1983.

eunuchs   castrated men who were officials in the Emperor's court
potash   a potassium compound

In AD 1907 the scientist Aurel Stein (AD 1862–1943) was able to confirm that paper had been invented in AD 105 when he came across a remnant of an early part of the Great Wall of China and found a sealed bin in what must have been an ancient watchtower. Nine documents in the bin were written on paper made from rag fibres. The documents were dated to within 50 years of Cailun's famous discovery. In source 7.3, Stein describes a further discovery at Dunhuang.

7.3

Discovering manuscripts

… on its door being opened by the priest, I caught a glimpse of a room crammed full to the roof with manuscript bundles … The sight of the small room was one to make my eyes open wide. Heaped up in layers, but without any order, there appeared in the dim light of the priest's little lamp a solid mass of manuscript bundles rising to a height of nearly ten feet.

Aurel Stein.

女 + 馬 = 媽 **7.4**

female person + mǎ = mā (mother)

Writing about history

Imagine you have been asked to explain the process of papermaking. In a short report give a background to the development of writing and explain how paper is made.

Chinese art and architecture

Chinese art uses a large number of symbols. Horses symbolise high rank while water buffalo represent the peasant's life of toil. Mandarin ducks represent a happy marriage and a tiger is a symbol of virility. The dragon represented the Emperor and the phoenix was a symbol of the Empress.

Stone was first used in the Han period. 'Spirit roads' of stone figures guarding the way to a tomb became common from the first century.

In the medieval period, art was seen as a form of pleasure but from early times it often also had a practical function. Artists of the Shang period produced beautiful bronze works that had a practical use. Shang bronze pieces were used for cooking or storing food, for drinking or for religious purposes. Chinese art, from the Shang period until today, shows a willingness to borrow from other **cultures**.

culture   ideas, customs and art of a society
ceramic   clay heated to a high temperature

Designs were introduced into bronze ware during the Zhou Dynasty. **Ceramic** ware was developed in the late Zhou period. Both jade and bronze artwork lost their earlier symbolism and were used as decorations.

Painting on scrolls of silk was popular. In the Song Dynasty the most famous paintings were of landscapes.

In the Yuan and the Ming dynasties architecture flourished. Some of the finest examples from this period include the Temple of Heaven and the Summer Palace in Beijing, and the Imperial Palace in Nanjing.

Dyes made from flower or herb extracts were used. In the early dynasties each family dyed its own material.

7.5

Bronze vessel from the Shang period

Porcelain

Pottery had been made by the Chinese since Neolithic times. Porcelain was made with white China clay mixed with powdered **feldspar** and although it was used earlier, there is no recorded mention of porcelain till the seventh century (AD 600s).

There are different qualities of porcelain, and the finest was always reserved for the Emperors. Ming porcelain is a mixture of **kaolin** clay and Chinese stone, which when fired at 1400°C produces a material that cannot be scratched by steel.

feldspar	a hard mineral found in igneous rock
kaolin	a fine white clay used to make porcelain

'Hoa-pei' or porcelain painters followed a tradition of painting flowers, or animals or landscapes. 'Crackle-ware' gives the impression of many fine cracks on the surface of items, such as bowls and vases. This effect is produced by the oil paint that the painter uses.

7.6

Silk scroll, Water and Moon **Kuanyin**, *Southern Song Dynasty (1127–1279)*

Poetry

Some of the most famous Chinese poetry was written during the Tang period. It spoke of personal experience and made social comment.

Old age

But now I'm pale and sallow
My hair ruffled by the wind, tinged grey by the mist,
I fear to go out at night
Better to hide behind the bamboo curtain
Listening to the laughter of others.

Li Qingzhao (1081–1155 AD)

Researching the past

Use the following web site as a starting point to find out more information about an area of Ancient Chinese art that interests you:
http://china.pages.com.cn/chinese_culture/culture.html

---

abacus   beads on metal rods contained within a frame, used as a counting device
astronomer one who scientifically studies the planets and other heavenly bodies
Kuanyin   goddess of mercy

Discoveries and inventions

Tea was introduced to the world by the Chinese. Some people claim it was being drunk as far back as 2737 BC, but it was certainly an established custom by the time of the Tang Dynasty in the seventh century (AD 600s) and a writer of the period, Lu Yu, wrote of the varieties of teas and the process of tea preparation and its rituals. The Chinese invented a tea shredder.

The spirit of inquiry and a need for practical aids for daily life led Han scientists to invent the hodometer, a machine that measured distance. They made a sundial that measured time. They made iron drills to drill bores and blast furnaces to use in making tools from iron.

The Chinese invented printing with wood blocks and moveable type and they also invented ink. The Chinese talent for invention saw the development of wheelbarrows for use in agriculture and also the mechanical clock. They invented the **abacus** to help in the process of counting and keeping records. They were also responsible for the development of leisure pursuits, such as chess, and were probably the first to make kites.

The royal **astronomer**, Zhang Heng, developed an earthquake detector (a **seismograph**) in AD 130. In the year AD 1054 the chief astronomer of the Song Emperor witnessed the end of a star. It was the explosion of a supernova in the Taurus constellation. It can still be seen today and is known as the Crab Nebula.

Other Chinese inventions were numerous. In the eleventh century BC they invented umbrellas. They also invented the fishing reel and improved transport by boat by inventing the pivoting needle compass and the rudder. The use of the compass in China was first recorded in AD 1119.

The Chinese used saltpetre in the eleventh century (AD 1000s) and had invented gunpowder, made from saltpetre, sulphur and charcoal, by AD 1044. The Chinese use of fireworks was known in the twelfth century (AD 1100s).

The water mill wheel was devised in China for irrigation. Later Chinese waterwheels powered **bellows** for metalworking.

Some people claim that wallpaper was invented in China and introduced to Europe in the sixteenth century (AD 1500s). Hand painted Chinese wallpaper known as 'India papers' were brought to Europe in the seventeenth century (AD 1600s).

It is said that the Yellow Emperor invented the cart, the boat and the south-pointing chariot, the laws of astronomy and the first calendar. The chariot had a gear mechanism that enabled a pointer always to indicate south no matter which way the cart turned.

Legend says Shennong, the Red Emperor, invented herbal therapy. Lei Zu, Huangdi's wife, taught the people to raise silkworms and weave beautiful silk fabrics; Cang Jie invented pictographs. Ling Lun invented the 12-tone musical scale and Li Shou invented various measuring instruments.

seismograph	an instrument that measures the length and intensity of earthquakes
bellows	a device with an air chamber that creates a directed stream of air

Medicine

The Chinese were also responsible for many discoveries and inventions related to medicine. The world's oldest textbook on medicine is the *Nei Jing*, the Yellow Emperor's *Classic of Internal Medicine*. It includes information on acupuncture. Acupuncture can be traced back to the Emperor Fuxi (approximately 3000 BC) who traditionally compiled the *Book of Changes* (*I Ching*) and involves using needles to stimulate certain areas of the body. The needles block or stimulate the flow of Yin and Yang into these areas.

Chinese doctors discovered the body's 24-hour cycle (the circadian rhythm).

By the time of the Tang Dynasty doctors had to pass exams. Chinese doctors used three different types of treatment:

* herbal cures (they used herbs such as star anise, Chinese parsley, ginseng, garlic)
* acupuncture (they believed there were twelve lines called meridians on the body)
* moxibustion (the doctor applied heated herbs called 'moxa' to an acupuncture point to relieve pain).

Using the information

1 Draw up a timeline showing ten Chinese inventions.
2 Which invention do you think was most important? Give your reasons.
3 Using the information in this chapter and your own research, prepare a short presentation on the subject of what ancient and medieval China has given to the world.

Acknowledgements

The author and publisher wish to thank the following for permission to reproduce material:

Cover White Tara, Nepal. Asian Art Museum of San Francisco, The Avery Brundage Collection, Chong-Moon Lee Center for Asian Art and Culture B60S22+

Figure 1.8 'Ancient Chinese Public Examination', watercolour and ink on silk. Bridgeman Art Library/Bibliotheque Nationale, Paris, France; **1.11** Scroll, 'The Kangxi Emperor inspects the building of a dyke'. The Art Archive/Musèe Guimet, Paris; **1.12** Photo: Macleay Museum/David Herbison-Evans; **2.4** British Library, London/Werner Forman Archives; **2.5** © Copyright The British Museum; **2.10, 5.4, 5.5, 5.6, 6.4** Robert Harding Picture Library, London; **3.6, 3.8** Gulistan Imperial Library, Tehran/Werner Forman Archives; **5.1** Photo: Gjyn O'Toole; **6.2** Werner Forman Archives; **7.5** Private Collection/Werner Forman Archives; **7.6** 'Water and Moon Kuan-yin' 13th – early 14th century. Hanging scroll, ink, slight color and gold on silk. The Nelson Atkins Museum of Art, Kansas City Missouri (Purchase: Nelson Trust).

Every effort has been made to trace and acknowledge copyright but there may be instances where this has not been possible. Cambridge University Press would welcome any information that would redress this situation.